D0842764

CLACKAMAS HIGH SCHOOL LIBRARY

Drug Abuse and Society™

KETAMINE
Dangerous Hallucinogen

The Rosen Publishing Group, Inc., New York

Brad Lockwood

To you, youth, our future

Published in 2007 by The Rosen Publishing Group, Inc.
29 East 21st Street, New York, NY 10010

Copyright © 2007 by The Rosen Publishing Group, Inc.

First Edition

All rights reserved. No part of this book may be reproduced in any form without permission in writing from the publisher, except by a reviewer.

Library of Congress Cataloging-in-Publication Data

Lockwood, Brad.
Ketamine: dangerous hallucinogen / Brad Lockwood.—1st ed.
    p. cm.—(Drug abuse and society)
Includes bibliographical references and index.
ISBN-13: 978-1-4042-0911-4
ISBN-10: 1-4042-0911-5 (library binding)
1. Ketamine—Juvenile literature.
I. Title. II. Series.
RD86.K4L63 2007
615'.782—dc22

                                                    2006012634

Manufactured in the United States of America

Contents

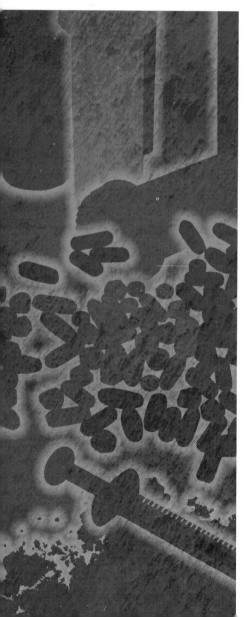

A former user, Rob, describes ketamine as a phantom drug. He says that one of the reasons that ketamine remains such a danger to users is because you can never be certain if what you have ingested is ketamine or a mix of drugs. He described ketamine's effects as "unpredictable," and says, "One time I felt like I was floating like an angel. The next time I became totally paralyzed and thought I was dying."

This description of ketamine, medically known as ketamine hydrochloride, is actually very common. Using ketamine is sometimes referred to as "entering the K-hole." Special K, as the drug is known on the street, produces sensations that make users feel disconnected from reality. In many cases, the drug makes users feel that

During high school, students may attempt to convince you to explore drugs at social events. Sometimes offered at late-night parties, ketamine is considered a dangerous hallucinogenic drug that causes the user to feel completely disconnected from reality.

they have died. Many former abusers like Rob admit to initially experimenting with ketamine and other club drugs, like GHB (gamma hydroxybutyrate), MDMA (methylene-dioxymethamphetamine, or ecstasy), and Rohypnol (flunitrazepam, the "date rape" drug), at all-night parties. But after a near-death experience—and the rape of a friend when she overdosed on ketamine—Rob quit using. He now wants to warn others about the dangers associated with ketamine and other club drugs.

Because ketamine is an anesthetic (a drug that causes a loss of sensation, especially to pain), it makes users feel drunk, relaxed, euphoric, and almost dreamlike. This made it one of the most popular party drugs of the 1990s. But these same side effects (and regular mixing with other drugs) also make it one of the most dangerous. Long-term ketamine abusers experience mental problems and may sometimes experience visual impairment. Abusers may also end up with felony arrest records for trying to buy ketamine, steal it, or push it on others. No longer a common street drug, ketamine has been classified as a Schedule III drug under the Controlled Substances Act since 1999, and it is thereby restricted for use by physicians and veterinarians only.

Even more dangerous is the effect of ketamine on innocent victims. Since the drug is an anesthetic, its results vary depending on the amount that is used and the weight of the person ingesting the drug. Unsuspecting ketamine users often experience degrees of paralysis, confusion, and even unconsciousness, making them vulnerable to strangers and sexual aggressors. Occasionally, people never intending to use ketamine have it slipped into their drink or "laced" into a cigarette or marijuana joint. The resulting trip can cause paranoia, and the person may become a victim of sexual assault. This is why ketamine is sometimes referred to as a "date rape" drug.

Ketamine was developed in the early 1960s to sedate animals and humans for surgery. It is being used less for this purpose because faster, safer drugs are now available. Beginning in the 1990s, people began experimenting with ketamine, and its recreational use increased sharply. Imagine the confusion among police and medical professionals when animal clinics were being robbed of this tranquilizer. Why were people stealing ketamine?

As it turned out, ketamine was an ideal party drug. In its standard form as a powder, it looks like cocaine and is snorted. It can also be modified for injecting, smoking, or drinking. Ketamine users liked that the drug's effects were shorter in duration when compared to the hallucinogens PCP (phencyclidine) and LSD (lysergic acid diethylamide), and that it was only mildly addictive when compared to heroin, crack cocaine, and crystal methamphetamine. Ketamine users also learned that their bodies metabolized the drug faster than other hallucinogens and narcotics, making it harder to detect in urine and blood samples. Tragically, the effects of ketamine also made it popular among potential sexual aggressors and criminals, who could drop just a small amount of it into a stranger's drink and take advantage of his or her impaired mental state. As the illegal use of ketamine increased, instances of crimes like assault and rape also increased in frequency, especially in places where drug activity was higher.

CHAPTER 1

Societal Trends

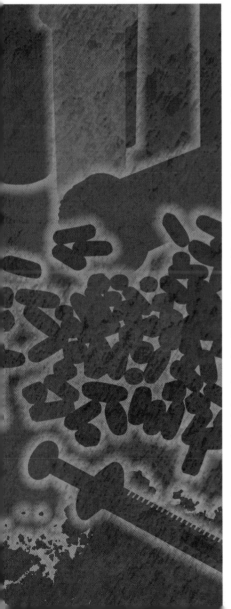

The 1950s and early 1960s were a period of dramatic pharmaceutical discoveries, which inevitably led to increased drug experimentation and abuse. Hallucinogens like LSD and PCP became some of the era's most popular drugs. Less known, but equally effective, was a drug synthesized by Belgian chemist Charles L. Stevens in 1962 called ketamine hydrochloride. Often considered close chemical cousins, PCP and ketamine were developed as anesthetics for animals and humans, allowing for painless surgical procedures while patients were awake and aware. By the mid-1960s, the pharmaceutical company Parke-Davis owned the patents to manufacture and market both PCP and ketamine.

Almost immediately, however, the two drugs were surrounded by controversy.

Scientists who sought to replace PCP (phencyclidine) with a less dangerous anesthetic first developed ketamine in the early 1960s as a drug for humans, but they soon realized that its effects were too unpredictable. Today, ketamine is primarily used to sedate animals for surgical procedures.

Sales of PCP were stopped because the drug's effects on patients proved to be too unpredictable. Some patients reported becoming confused while under the influence of PCP. Others became aggressive and even violent after the drug was administered. Instead of becoming relaxed and immobilized, patients experienced a variety of disturbing consequences, some of which eventually made PCP a popular, but illegal, street drug.

Ketamine was thought to be more reliable and milder than PCP. Soon, though, clinical tests showed that approximately 20 percent of patients given the drug claimed to experience a dreamlike state and, at times, hallucinations that they were dying.

PCP was made illegal. Yet because reports of problems among ketamine users were relatively infrequent (and because the drug was far more predictable than PCP), the Federal Drug Administration (FDA) officially approved ketamine for use on animals and humans in 1970. Today, ketamine is sold under the brand names of Ketaset, Ketanest, and Ketalar.

HOW KETAMINE WORKS

Ketamine targets two regions of the brain: the thalamus and hypothalamus. Both regions are very active while we are awake. The thalamus routes all senses from the rest of the body, while the hypothalamus regulates primary instincts and emotional responses. When ketamine is introduced into the brain, however, these regions are effectively shut down. This makes ketamine users feel detached, free of pain, and unable to react to external stimuli. Basically, ketamine makes the brain think the body is sleeping. Ketamine makes the brain unresponsive even though

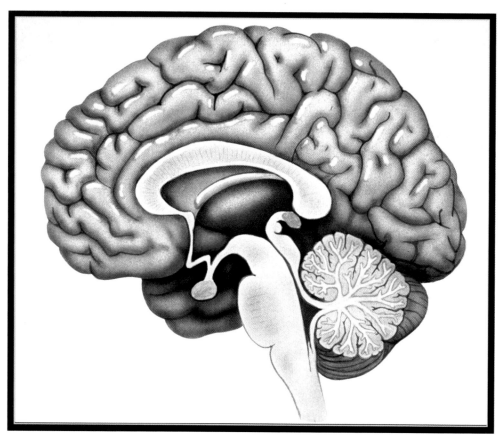

Like other anesthetics, ketamine acts on specific areas of the brain. The drug targets the thalamus and hypothalamus, and chemically dulls these areas so patients don't feel pain. Although ketamine is mostly used to sedate animals, it is still used for human patients in emergency situations when their medical history is unknown, such as when they are admitted while unconscious.

users are actually awake. In this state, when the brain is chemically blocked from communicating with itself or the outside world, the void is filled with visions, dreams, or memories. This process gives the user the sense of hallucinating or, when taken in larger doses, dying.

The effects of ketamine on the brain make it a potent anesthetic because patients feel no pain or discomfort while under its influence, and they won't move suddenly during surgery. However, these same effects also make ketamine attractive to abusers because they use the drug to achieve a surreal state. Immobilized and nearly paralyzed, large-dose ketamine users feel so relaxed that the drug-induced state represents a chemical escape from everyday life into a dreamlike realm.

EARLY EXPERIMENTATION

When used solely as an anesthetic, ketamine is effective; however, its hallucinogenic side effects soon made it a popular experimental drug. Interestingly, it wasn't dealers or long-term drug users who were ketamine's first abusers. It was actually medical professionals who were doing the experimenting. Like some doctors had done when LSD was invented, these physicians tried to expand their minds by using ketamine. Understanding that it was, in fact, approved for human consumption, ketamine was preferred among a few medical professionals who wanted to experiment with hallucinogens.

One of these early experimenters, D. M. Turner, was among the first ketamine fatalities. Turner was author of *The Essential Psychedelic Guide*. He conducted a round of tests on ketamine to determine its effectiveness, delving into near-death experiences for research purposes. The last time Turner pushed the bounds of ketamine, he was found drowned in his bathtub. Traces of ketamine were discovered in his bloodstream, and his death caused more serious concerns about the drug's use. At least seven known fatalities have resulted from ketamine overdoses since its invention.

MEDICAL, THEN MASS, USE

Ketamine is difficult to manufacture. It requires expensive laboratory equipment, time-intensive techniques, and an understanding of complex chemical reactions to synthesize the drug. For these reasons, ketamine is limited in its availability on the street. This helps control its abuse.

The use of ketamine as a human anesthetic steadily declined during the 1960s. This was mostly due to the discovery of safer anesthetics. Since that time, ketamine's use has been limited to anesthetic applications on cats and monkeys. Meanwhile, trends in drug enforcement indirectly led to a resurgence of ketamine abuse among people, especially teenagers.

Bans on LSD and PCP made these drugs unavailable legally and therefore more expensive when purchased illegally. Due to

This veterinarian examines one of her feline patients to determine its needs. Because ketamine is largely produced to serve veterinarians and their patients, people seeking large supplies of the drug to use or sell on the street sometimes vandalize animal clinics.

their difficulty to manufacture, most LSD and PCP available on the street were of poor quality or contaminated, and many users complained of never getting high. In the worst scenarios, users overdosed on LSD and PCP because other chemicals were hidden in the mixtures, creating lethal substances. Unfortunately, the widespread consumption of these synthetic drugs had made users more open-minded to other manmade drugs. Unlike marijuana, psychedelic mushrooms, and peyote, which are often considered organic because they grow naturally, users were now considering the highs attainable from synthetic chemical mixtures. Suddenly, they were more open-minded about popping pills, snorting powders, and injecting and/or smoking synthetic drugs. Ketamine was being experimented with once more.

Paralleling users' openness to alternative pharmaceuticals was a new drug scene altogether. As in the 1960s, drug use in the mid- to late 1990s was popular at social events, especially raves—all-night dance parties often held in secret locations. The loud music, bright flashing lights, and huge crowds required high energy, which made the use of stimulants like cocaine common, as well as hallucinogenic drugs like GHB, ecstasy, and ketamine.

THE IDEAL PARTY DRUG

The side effects of ketamine made it highly popular at parties. Small doses heightened the overall sensory experience, making the music and lights more intense and the people and surroundings more interesting. Ketamine's high is relatively short (usually one to two hours) when compared to that of LSD, PCP, or ecstasy, the effects of which can sometimes last for hours or days. The human body metabolizes ketamine rapidly, so within twenty-four to forty-eight hours, the drug is completely untraceable in urine or blood tests. It became the ideal club drug for infrequent use in small doses (just once or twice at a party or rave), and it started circulating with names like Special K, K, Kit Kat, and cat valium.

MYTHS AND FACTS

MYTH: Ketamine (Special K) is an organic substance like marijuana and mushrooms, so it's natural and safe to ingest.

FACT: Ketamine hydrochloride is a chemical manufactured in laboratories. Medical professionals use it to sedate animals and humans before surgery. It isn't natural or organic, and it isn't safe for casual use. Ketamine should only be administered by a doctor and used under a doctor's care and supervision.

MYTH: As long as I try only a little Special K with friends, I'll be fine.

FACT: Ketamine was developed for medicinal use and works well for its intended purpose. Because you never know how ketamine will affect you, it should not be taken unless a doctor administers it. Taking ketamine with friends is dangerous because you never know how much of the drug is too much. Also, because "friends" are often the first people to introduce you to powerful drugs, be careful of your associations and choose your friends with care.

MYTH: I don't take drugs, so I don't need to worry about ketamine.

FACT: Because ketamine has the potential to eliminate social inhibitions, sexual aggressors and criminals often slip it into someone's drink. Stay alert when you go out: According to the American Council for Drug Education (ACDE), 55 percent of female college students and 75 percent of male college students involved in acquaintance rape admitted to having been drinking or using drugs when the rape occurred.

Play it safe. Have fun dancing and partying, but consume non-alcoholic beverages like water and sports drinks to keep yourself properly hydrated. If you are of age, drink alcohol in moderation. And keep a close eye on your glass! If you suspect that your drink has been tampered with in any way, dispose of it immediately. While at social events, enjoy beverages from closed containers such as bottled water and canned soda. If you can't keep your drink with you at all times, drink it completely and then dispose of it. An open cocktail or beverage can sometimes lead to disastrous results for an unsuspecting person. In other examples, you should never enter into a situation where you are a passenger in a vehicle that is being operated by someone you suspect may have been drinking alcoholic beverages or using ketamine or other drugs.

According to a multi-year study completed in Hong Kong in 2001, more than 72 percent of ketamine use occurred at a dance club or bar. Obviously, ketamine had become a social drug. In the same study, 90 percent of users remarked that they took the drug with friends, while a scant 5 percent took it at home while alone. Clearly, ketamine and raves went hand in hand, and both catered to a young, impressionable group. Unfortunately, it wasn't long before ketamine was also associated with inebriating people before criminal activities such as rape or robbery.

Before long, people—usually females attending parties with no intention of taking drugs—became unknowing victims of abuse. Many women reported waking up in a confused state, finding that they'd been molested, assaulted, raped, or robbed. They were unable to remember exactly what had happened. These women felt paranoid and betrayed. To make matters worse, authorities in most cases were unable to test for ketamine intoxication because the drug metabolizes so rapidly. Besides being a popular party drug, ketamine was now the perfect date—or acquaintance—rape drug.

CHAPTER 2

Users and Pushers

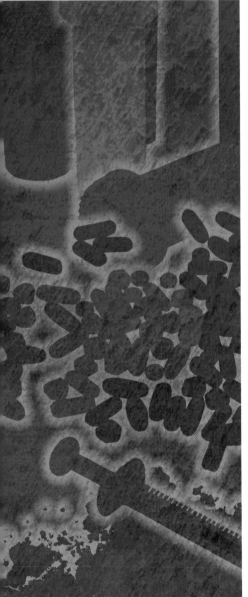

The vast majority of first-time drug users won't snort powders or inject themselves with needles. Upon introducing ketamine to the party scene, however, dealers and users often took advantage of the drug's generic physical appearance to get others to try it.

In its standard form, ketamine looks like a white powder similar to cocaine. This similarity makes it easier for dealers to pass it off as cocaine without the user knowing any better. Adding to ketamine's physical advantages among dealers is the fact that it can be modified into crystals that may be sprinkled into a tobacco cigarette or marijuana joint. Ketamine can also be changed into a liquid for drinking or injection. It can even come in a pill form that is often mistaken for ecstasy. Although ketamine is

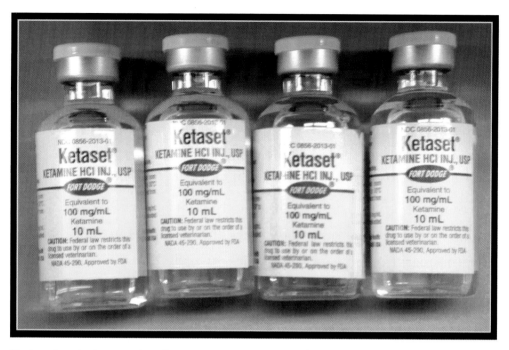

Ketamine is known by the commercial name Ketaset, and it is normally distributed to hospitals and clinics as a liquid that can be injected into the vein of a patient to anesthetize him or her for surgical procedures.

difficult to manufacture, its physical properties make it easy to disguise.

Even when not presented as, or mixed with, another drug, ketamine has taken on a certain mystique. Instead of being described accurately as a controlled substance for serious medical procedures, ketamine quickly developed a false mythology on the street. Dealers claimed that it was less potent than it truly was. Rumors spread that ketamine was an organic substance that was discovered in the jungles of South America. Some people falsely believed indigenous tribes used it for sacred ceremonies. Ketamine was

21

gaining a false reputation as a "safe" drug, which made many people more comfortable when trying it for the first time.

Such myths, as well as seemingly innocent nicknames, helped make ketamine popular among teenagers. Had they known that the drug was purely chemical and developed only in laboratories as an anesthetic for humans and animals, some may not have tried ketamine at all. However, its chemical properties, and the fact that its high is brief and it quickly disappears from the body, made it a favorite among both users and dealers. Further, the extreme markup in illegal ketamine—usually $20 per "bump" (0.2 grams)—made it highly attractive to dealers looking for increased profits.

Users of ketamine were eager for a drug that promised a quick high and that could not be traced. They could dance for hours and then leave a rave with only mild lapses in memory the following day. Other users reported feeling paranoid. Dealers promoted these supposed advantages of the drug, and all too soon, it was rare for a dealer at a rave not to have Special K for sale.

FIRST-TIME USERS

Teenage boys were often the first to try ketamine. They were also the primary dealers of the drug. Average first-time users were sixteen years old, while the average dealer was just one year older. Some ketamine users started as young as twelve, with very few trying the drug after twenty-eight years of age. Ketamine had developed a teenage following. Teens could be counted on to convince their peers to give the drug a try.

Ketamine quickly gained popularity because it was being distributed and sold by teenage dealers—friends endorsing the drug and selling it to other friends. Inexperienced, most of these first-time dealers and users did not know how much ketamine to take, or when they'd taken too much. This ignorance often led to bad trips or overdoses. Of even greater concern was the fact that first-time users often took ketamine thinking it was another drug entirely. In other cases, they took it in a combination of several drugs. According to the federal Drug Enforcement Agency (DEA), 75 percent of ketamine users also experimented with other drugs, dangerously mixing powerful chemicals. This mixing of drugs is called polydrug behavior, and it often leads to unpredictable and disastrous results.

When taken by itself, ketamine is not overly addictive (52 percent of long-term abusers cited symptoms of withdrawal in the previously mentioned 2001 Hong Kong study), nor is it highly lethal when compared to other drugs like heroin or PCP. But taking a variety of drugs, as ketamine users often did, resulted in chemical reactions that were highly risky and sometimes fatal.

MORE USE, MORE RISK

Because ketamine is a highly potent drug, taking too much can bring about unpredictable and dramatic results. Equally important

Teens may persuade their peers to try drugs for the first time. Usually, they will encourage them to experiment with drugs because "everyone else does." It's important to realize that people who try to get others to take drugs usually have a personal motive for doing so, like making money.

are the size and weight of users. These factors have a direct relationship to the drug's effect on them. The smaller the user, the smaller the dose required to get high.

Assuming a teenager is of average height and weight, a few snorts of ketamine powder or puffs of a ketamine-laced marijuana joint roughly equal a small dose (10–40 milligrams) of the drug, causing the user to feel drunk. At this stage of intoxication, colors blend, and vision and speech are distorted. Users report a sense of heightened awareness, while their body feels energized and their mind feels relaxed. Being under the influence of small amounts of ketamine makes you feel as though you are floating. Dancing in a large group while under the drug's influence is often described as a drunk and dreamy state of mind. Sounds, lights, and other visuals intensify, and thoughts become euphoric.

Take a larger dose (50–80 mg) of ketamine, however, and your body will totally relax. Your senses will begin to shut down as the chemicals impact your brain's thalamus and hypothalamus regions, and you will feel the need to sit down or lay back. Many users experience breathing difficulties when taking this much ketamine. Others become physically sick and some will vomit. At this stage, it is common to feel immobilized—you're unable to talk or see correctly. Other effects of a higher dosage can include the following:

- Visual distortions
- Lost sense of time and identity

- Confusion
- Ability to smell and taste is impaired
- Visual perception and sense of touch are more sensitive
- The sensation of floating away from your body
- Numbness in your extremities

An even greater dose of ketamine (more than 80 mg) will cause amnesia and unconsciousness. This is known as being in a K-hole. At this point, many users say it feels as if they've died, and they are highly vulnerable to themselves and to others. Effects of 80 mg or more of ketamine include:

- Increased heart rate
- Feelings of being paralyzed
- Visual and auditory hallucinations
- Numbness
- Impaired attention and memory
- Impaired learning abilities and motor functions
- Delirium and amnesia
- High blood pressure
- Respiratory depression and potential respiratory failure

It is the danger of using ketamine at higher doses that has created the most alarm about the drug. Having difficulty breathing, going in and out of consciousness, feeling your heart rate increase, and being paralyzed are incredibly terrifying experiences, especially if you are not expecting to be drugged. Even if ketamine is taken willingly, it is impossible to know how it will affect you. At higher doses, many users scratch or injure themselves without knowing it. Worse, others may be assaulted, robbed, or raped while under the influence of the drug. Simply put, ketamine incapacitates. Paralyzed, unable to move or feel, confused, and at times unconscious, users are highly vulnerable to sexual aggressors and other criminals.

KETAMINE AND CRIME

As the use of ketamine became more widespread at parties, particularly at raves, so did assault and rape. Again taking advantage of the physical and chemical properties of the drug, assailants slipped it into the drink of an unsuspecting victim or laced it into another drug. Before victims realized it, they were suddenly immobilized without any way to defend themselves.

Another synthetic drug, flunitrazepam, sold under the trade name Rohypnol and better known on the street as "roofies," was also being used by sexual predators and other criminals. Like ketamine, Rohypnol immobilizes the body and incapacitates unsuspecting victims for assault and/or rape. Far more prevalent than ketamine, Rohypnol brought increased attention to the illegal use of drugs to facilitate sex crimes in the mid-1990s.

Beyond its potential for abuse, ketamine also incited an unexpected string of crimes during the same time period. Because ketamine must be commercially manufactured, it is hard to obtain. Illegal trafficking from Mexico, and later China, supplied most dealers, but the original market for the drug made for a most unusual series of robberies. Animal clinics, veterinary offices and suppliers, and even offices of the Society for the Prevention of Cruelty to Animals (SPCA) were being broken into, confusing law enforcement personnel across the country. Several arrests in California, Connecticut, New Mexico, and Oklahoma revealed what these uncommon criminals had in common. They were all stealing ketamine for street distribution.

Because of the rise in prescription drug abuse, many pharmacists may be obligated by law or by the rules of their employers to secure narcotics and other dangerous drugs within locked safes, drawers, and cabinets. For similar reasons, many veterinarians also keep ketamine supplies in locked containers.

How Ketamine Gets to Abusers

Ketamine is primarily available through illicit means. Street sales are rare, making alternative distribution methods the only way to obtain the drug. Because it is often bought over the Internet and imported from suspect veterinary distributors and clinics, ketamine often travels thousands of miles before reaching abusers. According to a 2004 bulletin from the U.S. Department of Justice, law enforcement officials reported the following illicit sources of the drug:

- Belgium, China, Colombia, Germany, and Mexico are the major manufacturers of ketamine outside of the United States.
- Robberies of animal clinics fed illicit markets for ketamine in the 1990s, but strict enforcement has cut off this source, forcing dealers to turn to international drug traffickers.
- A Tijuana, Mexico, veterinary clinic was caught diverting legal orders of ketamine for illicit shipment into the United States via mail.
- In 2002, twenty individuals were indicted for smuggling ketamine from Mexico; the drug was ordered over the Internet and then transported across the border into San Diego for distribution throughout the United States.
- In 2002, 70,000 vials of ketamine were seized from a single illegal drug trafficking group in the United States, while an additional 195,575 vials were seized in Mexico.
- Missouri State Highway Patrol officers who pulled over a car in a routine traffic stop discovered 3,998 vials of ketamine that were believed to have originated in Mexico and were intended for sale in New York.

KETAMINE'S CONSEQUENCES

Sadly, ketamine use has long-term consequences. In most cases, the drug itself does not impair a person's physical or mental state for a long period. However, the actions that occur while a person is under the influence of the drug are the chief problem. Friends quickly become dealers and, sometimes, predators and convicts. It was for this reason that ketamine was included in the Drug-Induced Rape Prevention Act of 1996. Anyone using ketamine to take advantage of another person now faces up to twenty years in prison.

Still, it took several years for ketamine abuse to be fully understood and controlled. Since it was categorized as a Schedule III drug in 1999, stricter legal enforcement and greater diligence by veterinarians and drug distributors have been effective in curbing its abuse over the last few years. But recovery from ketamine addiction is far easier than overcoming the mental and emotional problems associated with assault and rape. Many victims are still struggling with painful memories of being taken advantage of while under the drug's influence. U.S. law enforcement data shows that, on average, 2 percent of teenagers in grades 8–12 used ketamine in 2002. Ketamine use declined sharply in 2003, dropping by 20 percent, but many indictments and massive drug busts suggest that other, alternative sources are readily available to users.

CHAPTER 3
Human Behavior and Addiction

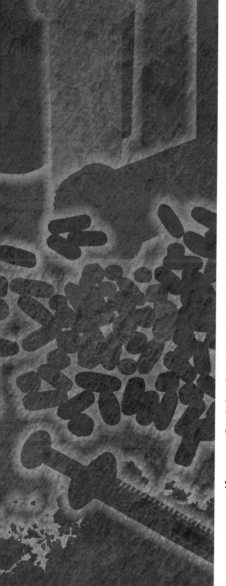

Sarah first tried ketamine at a rave in an old warehouse by the river. Her decision to go was influenced by her friends. They told her that the rave was going to be a chance to experience something really different. It was already past her curfew, but Sarah was too curious to miss what her friends were calling the experience of a lifetime.

The locations of raves have to be kept secret to keep the cops away, so the night started like most others. Sarah met her friend Jenna earlier for some quick food at their favorite spot. Sarah didn't think anything out of the ordinary would happen that night, maybe a movie or just driving around.

Then Jenna's friend Tye showed up, saying that he had a lead on a "killer

In many cases, teenagers who try drugs like ketamine do so because their peers pressure them to experiment with illegal substances. According to the National Survey of Substance Abuse Attitudes taken in 2001, 10 percent of teenagers have been to a rave where drugs like ketamine were "readily available."

party." Tye asked if anyone else wanted to come along. Sarah wasn't driving; Jenna was. In addition to having a car and license, Jenna had a huge crush on Tye. The decision was made. Jenna and Sarah followed Tye's motorcycle, speeding and weaving down dark roads until they came to a parking lot. Once there, Tye jumped off his bike and jogged back to their car.

"Stay here. I'll be right back," he instructed. He headed toward a group of strangers. Nervous, Sarah asked Jenna if they should leave because Tye's behavior seemed strange. Jenna wanted to stay. Watching what was going on, Sarah soon saw Tye turn and run back to their car. "I got the spot. Let's go!"

That's all Tye said, leaving them to continue following him on his motorcycle. They drove past another corner, losing Tye's taillights for a minute and then catching up again. Finally, they saw that they were headed to the old abandoned warehouse near the river.

TAKING PART IN SOMETHING BIG

The promised "killer party" was under way. Jenna was ecstatic and even Sarah was intrigued. She'd never been to a rave before, but dozens of people her age were entering the big, dark warehouse. Stepping out of the car, Sarah immediately felt the ground shake from the booming bass of the music inside.

Tye and Jenna entered the warehouse side by side and Sarah followed. They were amazed by the sight of laser lights firing blue and red beams across the gigantic room that was filled with hundreds of people. The music was loud and intense, and the DJ excited everyone, spinning beats and accepting requests with shouts. Joining the group, Sarah was enveloped in her first rave.

"Here, try this," said Tye, and Sarah turned to see him and Jenna smoking a joint. Sarah had tried marijuana before, laughing too much one time then falling asleep the next, so she declined. Tye smiled and said, "Try it. It's a special joint."

Sarah then looked to Jenna, and when her friend nodded, as if to say it's OK, Sarah took the joint. After just a few puffs, though, she knew it was unlike any she had smoked before. The lights were soon streaking and slowing, the music raged in her ears, the vocals grew clear and close, and her body started to tingle all over. It felt amazing, as if she were in a trance. Feeling the music pulse, each song seeming to last for hours, and her thoughts and heart were racing. Tye offered Sarah another puff, but she said no—this felt just right. The crowd was connected. Everywhere she saw strangers as friends. Everyone was there together, and she felt that she was a part of something important. Sarah had never felt so inspired before.

After a while, though, the positive feelings faded. The music and crowd remained, but Sarah felt tired and a bit depressed. She wanted to leave, and thankfully, so did Tye and Jenna. Walking back to the car, with Tye and Jenna now arm-in-arm, Sarah asked what made that joint so special.

"I added some Special K, that's what," Tye answered. Not knowing what he meant, Sarah asked what Special K was. Laughing, Tye explained, "It's cat valium. The Mayans used it during ritualistic ceremonies." Still confused but not wanting to seem stupid, Sarah didn't ask anymore questions. Tye and Jenna dropped her off at home.

SARAH'S NEW LIFE

Sarah's introduction to ketamine was the first of many times she used the drug. Tye and Jenna started dating and, because he always knew where to go, Tye had a new rave for them each weekend. Usually starting the evening with a meal, they would then go to another location to get directions and end up at an all-night party. The locations were always different but equally

Ketamine became popular in the 1990s as part of the growing club scene, which included all-night raves where drugs such as MDMA (ecstasy), GHB (gamma hydroxybyrate), and Rohypnol (the "date rape" drug) were often used by partygoers.

remote, and the scene was always the same: loads of people, loud music, and lots of Special K.

Having $20 and knowing what to ask for was enough. For her money, Sarah got little aluminum or paper packages of ketamine powder from Tye or just about anyone at a rave. No longer smoking ketamine, Sarah was now sniffing it and finding that she needed more to get high each time. To get the same floating and tingling feeling, she needed larger and more frequent doses. The first inhalation in both nostrils would get her high, making the colors streak and the music boom like before, but twenty minutes later she needed another "bump" to keep going.

The first time Sarah took too much K, she felt totally different. She couldn't taste or smell, and her thoughts were jumbled, almost lost, which was scary. But that euphoric feeling, of floating and being connected with everyone, eventually returned. The very idea of searching for drugs became an obsession: Her nights were spent finding the rave, finding some ketamine, finding the right high and maintaining it, then finding her way home the next morning.

The day after was always the worst, though, leaving Sarah exhausted and her memories distorted. She couldn't remember who she had danced with or how much ketamine she'd taken, and strange flashes of lights and thoughts would fill her mind. She felt on edge and paranoid, thinking that her parents knew what she was doing every weekend. Maybe Jenna told them. Could she trust her best friend? And why was that car always parked outside her house? Were people spying on her? Sarah wondered if maybe she shouldn't take drugs anymore. But thoughts of quitting would be gone by the next weekend.

SPECIAL CONNECTIONS

Tye always knew where to get ketamine, and he seemed to like Sarah. Tye and Sarah became closer. This made Jenna jealous, though, and she broke up with Tye and refused to go to anymore raves. Sarah still wanted to party, especially with Tye, so they started dating. Once Jenna found out, she and Sarah stopped speaking. Only months after that first rave, Sarah had lost her best friend and gained a boyfriend with whom she shared a "special" connection.

Over time, the raves began to blur together—dozens, fifty or so, each one the same—entering happy and eager, buying and using some K, then waking up depressed and paranoid. As bizarre as it may seem, Sarah got used to this routine—until Tye got arrested, that is.

He swore it was only for selling weed, but the felony charges stated otherwise. Tye's parents refused to bail him out, and a week went by without word. Sarah felt sick the entire time and became extremely depressed, withdrawn, and physically weak. Suddenly, she was without her boyfriend and supplier. She was lost. She needed more K.

Sarah started her search at her favorite restaurant, but skipped eating because Jenna arrived with her new friends. Jumping in a car with some people she knew from other raves, Sarah rode around until they found that weekend's location: it was the same old warehouse where she had experienced her first rave. Although her stomach was empty and growling, she entered the warehouse far hungrier for fun and a ketamine fix.

WELCOME TO THE K-HOLE

Sarah thought she knew the scene. Many of the faces looked similar, and she found another dealer quickly. He didn't have any K to smoke or snort, though. He only had liquid K, so Sarah would have to inject herself with a needle. She had always been afraid of needles, but her body needed this. Her mind raced as the needle entered her arm, her eyes staring as the clear fluid entered her bloodstream. And then it hit—ZOOM!

Sarah's heart was pounding. She tried to talk but couldn't form the words. It felt like her lungs had failed so she gasped, and then suddenly she couldn't move. Frozen, she fell against the wall and slid downward, staring up at her new friend but seeing his face change from a friendly smile to an evil mask, his eyes huge and his mouth like a dark cave. He seemed to be made of liquid. His face was flowing, changing forms, morphing in size and shape. Sarah started to panic. She heard him say, "Welcome to the K-hole, baby. Relax, breathe. You're in the K-hole, just relax and breathe . . . "

As his words filled her brain, Sarah started to float above the floor, fading upward until she swore she could see herself lying on the floor, strangers surrounding her, moving closer. She felt smothered, confused, and nearing blackout. All Sarah knew was that she was dying.

LEARNING THE UNTHINKABLE

Sarah awoke in an emergency room. Laying on a cold steel gurney, she stared at the ceiling. Flashes from the following night filled her head. She remembered that evil mask, bright lights, and unfamiliar hands touching her. She turned and saw her clothes on a chair beside her. Her shirt was covered with blood, and her jeans were ripped as if torn off her body. Pain shot up her arms, and she lifted them to see each one wrapped in gauze. Blotches of blood were stained through the gauze from her wrists to her elbows. Most of all, Sarah felt a deep ache coming from between her legs.

A doctor entered the room, busily taking notes. He finally looked up. "How are you feeling? Better now?"

"Where am I?" Sarah managed to mutter. "How did I get here?"

The doctor frowned then leaned close, placing a warm hand on her forehead. "A car dropped you off this morning," he said. "We don't know where they found you. They left right after they dropped you off. You were in bad shape."

"How bad?" Sarah had to know, feeling that ache between her legs.

Taking too much ketamine can subject you to serious health risks that include heart attack and respiratory failure. Although there have been few deaths directly attributed to ketamine abuse, there are countless accidents and injuries related to its use that are impossible to track by police officers and drug enforcement agencies.

"You were raped, it seems. I'm sorry," the doctor said, apologetically yet professionally, almost coldly. "We found your ID in your jeans and contacted your parents. They're on the way. Can you remember where you were last night? Do you remember taking any drugs? The police will need to ask you a few questions."

Sarah didn't answer. She couldn't. Her parents would know everything now. Was she pregnant? Would she get AIDS from that needle or the rape? Sarah had so many questions that she didn't dare ask. The doctor's stare made her feel even worse. What would the police do to her?

Still, she had to know what happened to her arms. Taking her wrists and lifting them, the doctor studied both of Sarah's arms, then her fingers. Frowning, he gently set them back down. "Sarah, you need to tell me what happened last night."

She couldn't answer.

The doctor continued. "When we found you, your fingernails were full of your own skin. Apparently, you were scratching yourself to the point of self-mutilation. Now, please answer me, did you do this to yourself?"

Staring at the ceiling, flashes of light and faint flickers of memories filling her mind, Sarah confessed, "Yes, I did."

GETTING HELP

Admitting you have a drug problem is the first step to a meaningful recovery. For Sarah, waking up in an emergency room was perhaps the only way to confront her ketamine addiction. Like many users, however, her mental wounds would take much longer to heal.

The first few weeks at the rehabilitation clinic were the worst. Sarah's physical withdrawal from ketamine included deep depression, a lack of appetite, and brief, infrequent flashbacks that also impaired her vision. For months, she wasn't even permitted to drive for fear that these flashes would cause her to crash. Even worse, she felt paranoid to the point of schizophrenia for several weeks afterward, thinking that people were talking about or spying on her. She felt that everyone was against her, including her doctors, parents, and friends.

Group therapy offered Sarah the best form of support. The most beneficial part of rehab was discussing what she was feeling with others who really understood. By talking and sharing her experiences with other users, Sarah didn't feel so alone. After one month of treatment, her body was fully recovered from addiction. But her arms will always bear the scars of her scratches, a common behavior exhibited by people who overdose on ketamine. The scars remain a constant reminder of her addiction.

STAYING CLEAN

Sarah's psyche remains equally scarred. Like many teenagers recovering from drug addiction, she was suddenly confronted with multiple issues. As a direct result of her abuse, she now had to deal with being raped. This would be the most intensive part of her recovery, demanding ongoing sessions with a psychiatrist that Sarah continues to see a decade later. She still finds it difficult to trust people, strangers especially, and she often blames herself for the rape. Earning back her parents' trust was easier than expected, but trusting herself remains difficult. This is a typical challenge for many former drug addicts.

Even today, Sarah finds that relationships are difficult to develop and maintain. She finds it hard to trust or to be intimate with anyone. Friendships are also fleeting because she doesn't think anyone will ever understand all she has been through. Sarah still regrets losing her best friend, Jenna, but doesn't miss Tye in the least. He got probation after he was released, but he was arrested again just a few months later. He served a long jail term for dealing controlled substances—cocaine and, of course, ketamine.

Interestingly and thankfully, other former abusers still offer Sarah the most help. Peers, those who are able to relate to using ketamine, offer her support when she is down. They help keep her from using drugs again. It is among this group of ketamine casualties that Sarah has found the greatest solace and strength. Sometimes, the only true friends that former addicts have are those who are also recovering from drugs. Recently, Sarah took the giant step of starting to date again, but she is taking things slow. She knows she has her whole life ahead of her, and she gives thanks for every day that she is clean and in control.

CHAPTER 4
Ketamine and the Legal System

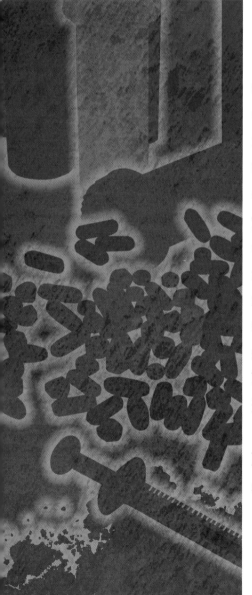

The history of ketamine as a synthesized medicinal drug parallels its enforcement as an illegal controlled substance. Approved by the FDA for use on animals and humans, experimented with by medical professionals, then disseminated through illegal means, ketamine is highly effective, yet mostly misunderstood. For years the dangers of the drug were largely overlooked. The very fact that it took nearly twenty-five years for it to be classified as a date rape drug, and several more to be closely monitored as a controlled substance, shows how slow the law has been to fully acknowledge the perils of its abuse.

Perhaps the greatest challenge facing law enforcement in controlling ketamine abuse is that the drug can have dramatic and unpredictable side effects. Compared to the rampant abuse of cocaine, crystal meth, and ecstasy, though, ketamine is often low on the list of law enforcement's concerns. Only when ketamine was tied to date rape did it receive the most attention, but even that recognition was short-lived because "roofies" got more notice.

Today, only six states monitor ketamine arrests, which makes any nationwide study of its abuse impossible. Meanwhile, the DEA includes ketamine busts and arrests with all other hallucinogenic drugs, including LSD, PCP, and GHB, which only complicates effective tracking. Nonetheless, the massive amount of hallucinogens seized each year highlights the need for greater diligence. The number of hallucinogens confiscated by the DEA nearly quadrupled in recent years, from 2,483,663 in 2004 to 8,425,499 in the first nine months of 2005. These numbers only reflect the amount seized. Just imagine how many doses were actually used!

While these statistics may show increased enforcement of existing laws leading to more seizures and arrests, the illegal drug trade continues. Federal drug enforcement agency officials admit that for every drug shipment seizure, at least four others reach their intended destinations. Moreover, the reality that licensed medical professionals, especially veterinarians and dentists, are abusing their access to ketamine to supply an illegal market shows how drugs can corrupt anyone. With widespread Internet access and so many errant dealers, ketamine use continues.

According to the U.S. Drug Enforcement Agency (DEA), ketamine is considered a Schedule III substance. Possession of a gram of ketamine can land you in jail for up to five years for a first offense.

STRONG DRUGS, STIFF PENALTIES

The DEA confronts drug trafficking with the same stance: the stronger the drugs, the stiffer the penalties. Rarely differentiating between a user and a dealer, mandatory sentences and fines are standard punishment, while rehabilitation is a lesser consideration.

Since ketamine is a Schedule III controlled substance, anyone caught with one gram or more faces up to five years in prison and a fine of up to $250,000. If caught again and convicted of the same crime, a person can be sentenced up to ten years in prison and be fined up to $500,000. In the legal system, the sole distinction between individual users and dealers, or illegal distribution networks, is in the fines. According to the DEA, if an institution, company, or corporation is caught possessing or selling drugs, the fines are automatically quadrupled. Whether or not this mandate is effective is open to debate, but such penalties do not go far enough to distinguish between individual users and the more serious criminals: drug dealers and traffickers.

Basically, the DEA has issued a blanket statement: If you are caught with drugs, whether to use yourself or to sell to others, you will be treated in the same way. In the end, small-time users are often sent to prison for the same number of years as dealers, pushers, and violent criminals.

Adding to the legal penalties of abusing ketamine is the fact that it actually incites other crimes, including breaking and entering into animal clinics (a misdemeanor), robbery (a felony, depending on the amount stolen), intention to distribute a controlled substance (a felony), and endangering the welfare of a child (a misdemeanor). As for those who use ketamine to assault and rape, the Drug-Induced Rape Prevention Act of 1996 requires up to twenty years in prison for a first offense. As a result, many people imprisoned for ketamine use are serving time for multiple crimes that are directly related to the drug and its dangerous impact on society.

BEYOND ENFORCEMENT

For all of the prison terms and fines, however, very few law enforcement mandates address the users' need for rehabilitation. Instead of being sent to one of the many clinics that offer rehab services, abusers are often sent to prison, where their addiction is never fully addressed. Once there, other drugs are plentiful, and prospects of a full recovery are slim.

As the DEA spends more money on fighting the spread of drugs, several studies have shown that actual use does not decrease proportionally. More often than not, alternative drugs become available to replace those being strictly enforced. For example, as police aggressively fight crack in cities, its use, as well as the use of similar drugs such as crystal meth, spreads throughout rural America.

The causes of drug abuse—the need to escape, lower inhibitions, or eliminate boredom—need to be the focus. In the end, only you can choose to stay off drugs. Once arrested, the law does not care why you possessed drugs, only that you did. If you choose to experiment, you must take responsibility for the consequences.

CHAPTER 5
Drug Abuse and Society: What Is the Impact?

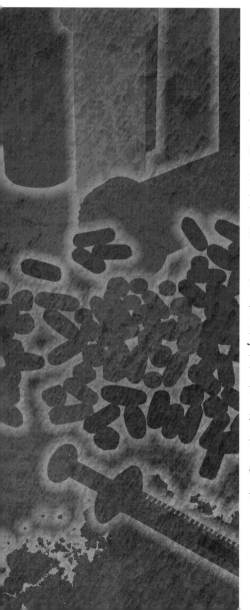

Every day, television commercials tout drugs as a solution for every ailment. In addition to individuals who may need medications, impressionable young people are being told that drugs can solve every problem. Drugs are abused rampantly in our society, whether they are legally prescribed by a doctor or are illegally purchased from a dealer.

Moreover, it is often medicinal drugs that are being abused, which makes young people more open to taking pills, just like many adults do each day. Repeatedly telling people that it's OK to use drugs will lead to increased use and abuse. The increased availability and advertisement of powerful prescription drugs can be directly tied to the increase in their abuse.

Young people, especially new drivers, should know that anytime they are pulled over by police for a traffic violation, they are at risk of having their vehicles searched. If the officer suspects the driver is under the influence of alcohol or drugs, or that a crime has been committed, your chances of getting searched are greater. In this instance, an officer is searching the trunk of a vehicle with a dog trained to find drugs.

Ketamine's impact on society is mixed. Veterinarians swear by its medical effectiveness, just as law enforcement and rape prevention authorities highlight its use to facilitate crimes. Evidence is offered from both sides. Although ketamine is associated with few long-term physical problems, its use is closely tied to high instances of rape and other criminal acts. Although few fatalities are associated with ketamine, victims have long-term mental problems from instances of assault and rape. Both sides have valid points, but getting all the information to young people has been slow.

Also lacking is effective, accurate tracking of ketamine arrests and abusers. The absence of law enforcement statistics about ketamine use also presents obstacles; lumping many drugs together and labeling them all as generically "bad" leaves professionals with no ability to judge the effectiveness of specific enforcement initiatives. Instances of using ketamine for assault and/or rape are equally untracked, making claims of a connection between the drug and crimes all too easy to make, but difficult to substantiate. As drugs become more complex and their use more widespread, authorities must make improvements in both tracking prosecutions and rehabilitating victims.

The increased abuse of ketamine in the 1990s should have been seen as a warning. It's a certainty that drug abuse undermines society, but are we taking the necessary steps today to limit future epidemics? Early education is critical, but the lack of statistics and information will continue to undermine our ability to accurately inform potential users and reform abusers.

CHAPTER 6

Ketamine and the Media: Epidemic or Distortion?

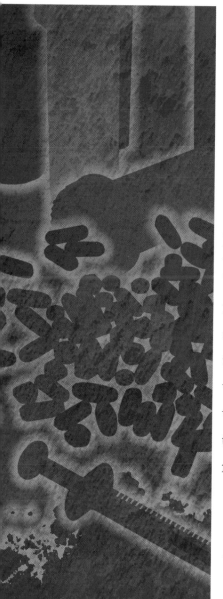

Ketamine abuse was indeed an epidemic in the 1990s, but it never received due notice; cocaine, crystal meth, heroin, and ecstasy continue to make the headlines. Even in the 1980s, as America was inundated with stories about adults abusing crack cocaine, no one was paying attention to large groups of teenagers experimenting with ketamine. Then, in the 1990s, ecstasy and "roofies" stole the headlines. Today, crystal meth is doing the same. All along, as authorities and the general public are distracted, drugs such as ketamine remain virtually ignored. As a result, those most vulnerable to first-time use, particularly teenagers, remain underinformed of ketamine's real danger.

EDUCATION IS THE FIRST STEP

Very few newspaper articles, television reports, or full studies—
even by the DEA or other government agencies—exist about
ketamine. Those that do mostly present the drug as a date rape
facilitator. Ketamine's merits as a medicine and its relatively
low addiction and fatality rates are often overlooked, as the

At some point during high school, you will likely be informed about the
dangers of recreational drug use. Because experts believe that education
is among the best methods to discourage teenagers from using drugs,
some states insist upon teaching students about the risks associated with
drug abuse in health and physical education classes.

instances of assault and rape are occasionally overhyped to sway potential users. This creates its own distortion and only undermines a full understanding of ketamine as a drug, not to mention why so many medical professionals and abusers favor it.

Law enforcement authorities are fortunate that ketamine is so difficult to manufacture, making international illicit trafficking the sole source. If not for this, ketamine use and abuse would have spread, with greater access and lower cost. Still, it took the drug's connection to assault and rape to bring it to the fore, as well as the necessary enforcement, steeper sentences, and fines. In the end, it was not increased education that led to overall declines in ketamine abuse, but the basic complexity of making it.

Ketamine use has declined significantly across the country for all age groups. From 2002 to 2003, the U.S. Department of Justice reported that ketamine use among the critical group of users, tenth graders (when the vast majority of first-time use occurs), declined from 2.2 percent to 1.9 percent. Twelfth graders showed similar decreases in use, from 2.6 percent in 2002 to 2.1 percent in 2003. However, a recent jump in DEA seizures of hallucinogens—nearly quadrupling from 2004 to September of 2005—suggests that these drugs may again be growing in popularity.

Moreover, recent tests of ketamine may lead to a resurgence of use in the future. One medical study published in April 2005 showed that low doses of ketamine significantly reduced pain among patients being treated for severe burns, cancer, congenital heart disease, asthma, and trauma. Children have shown the most significant improvements from these small doses, aiding in their comfort and treatment. Another study has shown that ketamine may be beneficial to recovery from alcoholism, and yet another shows the same for heroin addicts. The medical community is building a stronger case for increased use of ketamine in controlled medical environments among humans, which will definitely lead to greater access and possibly more potential for its abuse.

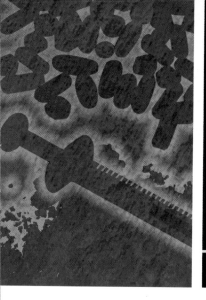

GLOSSARY

addiction A relapsing condition that is characterized by compulsive, irrational behavior and chemical changes in the brain.

anesthetic A drug used by doctors and surgeons to prepare patients for surgical procedures so they won't experience pain; anesthetics are usually administered by anesthesiologists.

euphoria A feeling of great happiness or well-being.

hallucinogen A drug that induces a dreamlike state of mind and that often produces abnormal visual or auditory effects.

hypothalamus A part of the human brain that regulates body functions such as temperature and certain metabolic processes.

ketamine hydrochloride A synthetic drug that was invented in the 1960s for use as an anesthetic for surgical procedures on animals and humans.

metabolize The act of fully processing a chemical, substance, food, or liquid through a person's body.

narcotic A drug that dulls the senses and induces sleep. Narcotics have the potential to become addictive with long-term use.

organic Something that is completely natural and not made by humans.

synthetic Something that is made by humans.

thalamus A part of the human brain that regulates sensations such as sight, hearing, taste, touch, and smell.

tolerance The degree to which a person's body is affected by a drug. A person who has been taking ketamine builds a physical tolerance to it in his or her body, meaning it will take more and more of the drug to make that person high.

withdrawal The mental and physical experience of detoxification a person goes through when he or she is no longer taking a drug after being addicted to it.

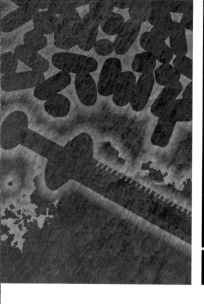

American Council for Drug
  Education
164 West 74th Street
New York, NY 10023
(212) 595-5810
Web site: http://www.acde.org

Canadian Centre on Substance
  Abuse (CCSA)
75 Albert Street, Suite 300
Ottawa, ON KIP 5E7
Canada
(613) 235-4048
Web site: http://www.ccsa.ca

Center for Substance Abuse
Treatment Information and

Treatment Referral Hotline
11426-28 Rockville Pike,
  Suite 410
Rockville, MD 20852
(800) 662-HELP
(800) 66-AYUDA (Spanish)
Web site: http://
  www.ncadi.samsha.gov

Community Anti-Drug
  Coalition of America
  (CADCA)
625 Slaters Lane, Suite 300
Alexandria, VA 22314
(800) 54-CADCA
Web site: http://
  www.cadca.org

Narcotics Anonymous (NA)
World Service Office in
  Los Angeles
P.O. Box 9999
Van Nuys, CA 91409
(818) 773-9999
Web site: http://www.na.org

National Clearinghouse for
  Alcohol and Drug
  Information (NCADI)
P.O. Box 2345
Rockville, MD 20847-2345
(800) 729-6686
(800) 767-8432 (Spanish)
Web site: http://
  www.ncadi.samsha.gov

National Council on
  Alcoholism and Drug
  Dependence (NCADD)
12 West 21st Street
New York, NY 10010
(800) 622-2255

Web site: http://
  www.ncadd.org

Teen Challenge of Southern
  California
5445 Chicago Avenue
Riverside, CA 92507
e-mail:
  info@teenchallenge.com
Web site: http://
  www.teenchallenge.com

WEB SITES

Due to the changing nature
of Internet links, Rosen
Publishing has developed an
online list of Web sites related
to the subject of this book.
This site is updated regularly.
Please use this link to access
the list:

http://www.rosenlinks.com/
  das/keta

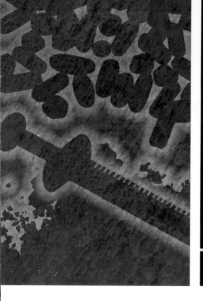

FOR FURTHER READING

Bayer, Linda N., and Austin Sarat. *Drugs, Crime, and Criminal Justice* (Crime, Justice, and Punishment). New York, NY: Chelsea House, 2001.

Fitzhugh, Karla. *Prescription Drug Abuse* (What's the Deal?). Portsmouth, NH: Heinmann Publishers, 2005.

Fooks, Louie. *The Drug Trade: The Impact on Our Lives* (21st Century Debates). Portsmouth, NH: Raintree-Heinmann Publishers, 2003.

Jansen, Karl. *Ketamine: Dreams and Realities.* Sarasota, FL: Multidisciplinary Association for Psychedelic Studies Publishers (MAPS), 2004.

Morgan, Hayley, and Justin Lookadoo. *The Dirt on Drugs: A Dateable Book.* Grand Rapids, MI: Revell, 2005.

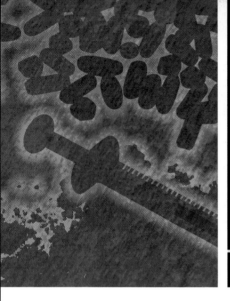

BIBLIOGRAPHY

Curran, H.V., and L. Monaghan. "In and Out of the K-hole: A Comparison of the Acute and Residual Effects of Ketamine in Frequent and Infrequent Ketamine Users." *Addiction*, 2001, Vol. 96(5): pp. 749-760.

Hong Kong Government. "A Study on the Cognitive Impairment and Other Harmful Effects Caused by Ketamine Abuse." Retrieved January 2006. (http://www.nd.gov.hk/ketamine-eng.pdf).

Dillon, P., J. Copeland, and K. Jansen. "Patterns of Use and Harms Associated with Non-Medical Ketamine Use." *Drug and Alcohol Dependence*, 2003, pp. 23-28.

Gahlinger, P. M. "Club Drugs: MDMA, Gamma-Hydroxybutyrate (GHB), Rohypnol, and Ketamine." *American Family Physician*, pp. 2,619-2,626.

Kent, James. "Ketamine: Metaprogramming from Within the Eye of the Storm." Retrieved January 2006 (http://www.erowid.org/chemicals/ketamine/references/other/1997_kent_resproject_1.shtml).

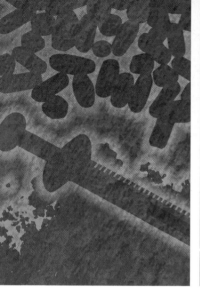

INDEX

Clackamas High School Library

ABOUT THE AUTHOR

Brad Lockwood is an award-winning author of several fiction and nonfiction books. His writings on politics and public affairs also regularly appear in national magazines and newspapers. As a father of a soon-to-be teenager, he appreciates the opportunity to write about various topics for young readers, educating students about drug abuse and addiction, government policy, and other timely subjects. Lockwood lives in Brooklyn, NY.

PHOTO CREDITS

p. 5 © B.S.I.P./Custom Medical Stock Photo; p. 10 © Andrew Brookes/Corbis; p. 12 © Alex Grey/Peter Arnold, Inc.; p. 15 © Bob Daemmrich/The Image Works; p. 21 Courtesy of the Drug Enforcement Administration; p. 24 © Mary Kate Denny/PhotoEdit, Inc.; p. 28 © Steinmark/Custom Medical Stock Photo; pp. 32, 46 © Michael Newman/PhotoEdit, Inc.; p. 35 © Mark Richards/PhotoEdit, Inc.; p. 40 © Pete Saloutos/Corbis; pp. 51, 54 © Bob Daemmrich/PhotoEdit, Inc.

Designer: Tahara Anderson; Editor: Joann Jovinelly; Photo Researcher: Marty Levick